Venusian In

Larry Sternig

Alpha Editions

This edition published in 2024

ISBN : 9789362929921

Design and Setting By
Alpha Editions
www.alphaedis.com
Email - info@alphaedis.com

As per information held with us this book is in Public Domain.
This book is a reproduction of an important historical work. Alpha Editions uses the best technology to reproduce historical work in the same manner it was first published to preserve its original nature. Any marks or number seen are left intentionally to preserve its true form.

VENUSIAN INVADER

By LARRY STERNIG

Leah Barrow would die. Tar Norn had sworn she would, unless he was set free. But freedom for the Venusian Pirate meant death for many, and it was Director Barrow's duty to hold him—even though it would cost his daughter's life.

Mart Wells shut off the alarm buzzer and jumped out of bed—much to his regret. He cussed and then grinned sheepishly as he brought up with a thud against the fortunately unbreakable glass of the window. A year on Callisto, and he could still forget that he weighed only thirty-six pounds and couldn't take a normal step without neutronium-weighted shoes.

Regaining his balance, he yawned and looked out over the rough Callisto landscape beyond Comprotown. Then he yawned again and reached for his uniform.

A year before, Comprotown—and his job as rocketport dispatcher—had been Romance with a capital R. Now, he thought gloomily, Romance with Leah with a capital L, and a fat lot of good that did him when Leah Barrow's father was Old Fish-face himself, Director of Comprotown.

True, Comprotown held fewer than a thousand colonists, but it was the only inhabited spot on bleak Callisto, and its Director was practical czar of a world. Yes, the Director could well afford to look down his long nose at any uniform with fewer than six stars on its right sleeve. But Leah didn't feel that—

Suddenly, straightening up as he fastened his weighted boot, he looked more intently out of the window. Something that flashed caught his eye out in the barren, warped hills. A gleam of metal where metal shouldn't have been. And it looked like a small spaceship.

Mart hastily pulled on his other boot and ran down the stairs. A red-headed mechanic from the rocketport was coming out of the building across the way.

Mart called out, "Red! Something about a mile back in the hills looks like a spaceship. Has one been reported down?"

"Huh?" The mechanic looked startled. "You sure? No, there hasn't been a report. Wait, I'll radio Central Communications."

He darted back into the building, and emerged a moment later. "No report. They're going to send out the autogiro to look at it. Say, Mart, there are only two small spaceships on Callisto. Could it be—"

Mart was already running toward the corner from which he could see the landing field. He stopped so suddenly that the mechanic almost ran into him, and said, "Whew! They're both there." Leah Barrow's trim little spacecruiser was safe in port. So was the Police one-seater scout—but that wasn't the one Mart had looked for first.

From near the Administration Building a two-place autogiro was rising, silhouetted for a moment between the horns of the reddish crescent of big Jupiter just above the horizon.

As he walked across the field toward headquarters, Mart surveyed the familiar scene. Three squat freighters were up on the racks, their ugly black bottoms over the ash-filled blasting pits; four others were on dollies ready to be serviced.

All seven were ready for their regular weekly Callisto-Jupe hop, ready to pick up more ore. And, as usual, they'd go out today to clear the field for the sleeker, faster, long-haul ships that would arrive from Earth tomorrow for the smelted metal. Mart glanced at his wrist-chronometer. Eight o'clock now; in an hour and a half, *Freighter One*, right on schedule, would start testing its rocket tubes for the ten o'clock hop. And an hour later, *Freighter Two* would start to warm up for the eleven o'clock blasting-off. And then the others, every hour on the hour.

At his desk in the Administration Building, Mart picked up the familiar sheaf of clearance papers waiting for his attention, and glanced through them. Initialing them was mere routine; they'd never cleared a minute early or a minute late since he'd been there. Director Barrow saw to that.

The door opened. Mart put down the papers and glanced up.

One of the workmen from the smelting plant, a tall black-haired fellow wearing tinted glasses, stood looking into the office. Mart didn't remember ever seeing him before—but with several hundred workmen, you couldn't remember all of them.

"Director Barrow in?"

Mart glanced up at the wall clock before he answered. "He'll be here in twenty-one minutes. Sit down and wait if you're off duty."

He turned back to the papers and finished initialing them, grinning inwardly at being able to say that the Director would arrive in twenty-one minutes exactly. It wasn't everywhere that one could make so accurate a prediction about anyone's arrival time, but Barrow was something of a chronometer himself.

He tossed the papers toward the back of the desk and threw the switch of the communicator on his desk, leaned forward slightly. "Dispatcher Wells calling Police Autogiro."

"Autogiro, Captain Wayne," came the reply. "Go ahead. Mart."

"I was the one who reported seeing the spaceship, Cap—if it was one. Found it? If not, I can—"

"Thanks, Mart, but we've sighted it all right. We're now circling, looking for a spot to come down. It doesn't take much, but damned if we can perch on a ridge like a canary. Neither could that space-speedster down there."

"Wrecked? What's it look like?"

"Ummm. Offhand one of the single-place jobs that Venusians bought from Earth before the war. Full armament, too."

"What? You sure, Cap? After the Earth-Venus twenty-two eighty treaty, we reclaimed and destroyed all the armed—"

"Yeah, I know," cut in the Captain's voice. "All but a few that the Venusian renegades—the pirates—got off with before then. Well—we're going down. Corey's found a place not too far from it where he can set the giro down, or says he can."

"If that's a pirate ship, Cap, be careful!"

"Don't worry. We're armed. And the ship's pretty smashed up. Probably at least kayoed whoever was in it. Well, keep your key open and I'll call you back. We're down."

Mart found the shipment chart and began to check off tonnage. That much he wanted to get out of the way before—but something was gnawing at the back of his mind. It took him a moment to trace what it was. Of course. The workman who was waiting for the Director was wearing tinted glasses.

Tinted glasses on Callisto! It didn't make sense. The sun, half a billion miles away, gives only a twenty-fifth of the light that falls on Earth. Even when that light is augmented by Big Jupe, it isn't—Yes, it was the first time he'd seen tinted glasses in Comprotown.

Curiously, he turned to glance at the seated workman. But the carrier wave of the desk communicator hummed and he forgot his visitor as Captain Wayne's voice boomed in.

"Dispatcher Wells. Captain Wayne calling Dispatcher—"

"Okay, Cap. Go ahead."

"We've examined the spaceship. No one's in it, hurt or otherwise. It's a single seater. A pirate ship all right."

"You sure? How can you be certain?"

"Aside from the fact that it would have no business around here if it wasn't, the papers are a give-away. There's a whole sheaf of them. Reports on the Ganymede jewel shipments mostly. And a full set of data on our own little world, Mart. If there's a Venusian around, he sure knows his way."

"Dope on Callisto? What kind?"

"A detailed map of Comprotown, showing every building. A full schedule of freighter hops both ways to Jupe and Earth. Details of shipments. That sort of thing."

"Holy stars! But why should a pirate be interested in ore?"

"Don't imagine he is. Or in Comprotown, either. I'd say from the papers, it was precautionary information. We don't keep our operations a secret here. He could have picked it up from any magazine article describing Comprotown in detail.

"But I still don't see—"

"The Ganymede jewel shipments, Mart. I'd say he was bound for Gany and his ship went blooie while he was scudding past Callisto. He got pulled down here and just barely made a landing he could walk away from. I'm afraid there'll be trouble."

Mart whistled. "Well, the Director's due now. He'll want a search organized and—Wait, here he is. Tell it over again, Cap, and you'll be reporting direct.... Listen to this, Director."

The tall slender figure of Director Barrow stood impassively beside Mart's desk and listened to a repetition of Wayne's report. Not a flicker of expression passed over his gaunt face.

As Wayne finished, the Director asked, "Is he armed? Anything taken from the ship's equipment, Captain?"

"Looks intact, but he probably has sidearms. All the pirates carry them. One funny thing, Director. The timer robot has been removed from the control panel. What on Callisto would he want with a loose timer?"

"Report back to headquarters immediately, Captain Wayne," Director Barrow ordered.

The hum of the carrier wave died and Mart clicked off the set. Then, belatedly, he stood up and saluted. "Anything I can do, sir? Everything's set for the freighters to clear as usual, so I'm more or less free—"

Barrow nodded. "Very good, Wells. You may go to the field and direct a search of the freighters. The Venusian's first thought will be to get away, and he may already be stowed in one of—"

A dry voice interrupted from behind the Director's back. "But the Venusian would not do anything so obvious, Director Barrow."

Mart whirled around. Barrow turned slowly and with dignity.

It was the tall man dressed in the uniform of a smelting plant worker who had spoken. But he wasn't dark-haired any more. Still seated, he was smiling at them sardonically as he fanned himself with a black wig he had just removed. The top of his head was as smooth as a billiard ball, and dead white. There was a line of demarcation where the dye he had applied to his face came to an end.

He had removed the tinted glasses too, and the blank-surfaced gray eyeballs showed why they had been worn. Now that the simple disguise of wig and glasses was removed, Mart noted some of the other distinguishing features that marked the Venusian. The general flatness of the face and flat unconvoluted ears. The six-fingered hands that had probably been thrust into the pockets of the stolen uniform.

The Venusian glanced down at the wig and glasses. "Standard equipment," he explained. "I always carry them in my ship and they've come in handy before."

He rose and bowed mockingly. "My name is Tar Norn, and your supposition that I am a pirate is correct. But I assure you that my visit here is accidental and I have no designs on Comprotown."

Tar Norn! The most vicious and notorious of the pirates, and the most ruthless killer of them all. Mart hastily jerked open the drawer of his desk and pulled out a hand-blaster. He started the formula: "Under authority of the Interplanetary Council, I arrest you, to be held for trial—"

The sardonic smile did not fade from the pirate's thin lips. He rose and extended his arms upward. "I am unarmed," he cut in. "It will help our discussion if you will verify that."

"—before the Supreme Council on Earth," Mart finished. Then, glancing side-wise at Director Barrow and seeing him nod, he stepped forward warily. Venusians, he knew, were both fast and tricky. Watching every move, he completed the search. Tar Norn carried no weapons.

Why, Mart wondered, had the pirate walked openly into headquarters and given himself up? Obviously, Tar Norn had something up his sleeve. But—

Director Barrow spoke coldly, as Mart stepped back, still covering the Venusian with the blaster. "Tar Norn, you speak of 'our discussion.' There is nothing to discuss. You will be sent to Earth."

The pirate's face became vicious. "I do not think so," he snapped. "I have taken a hostage. It was quite dark—your tiny Callisto in eclipse of its huge primary—when I was forced down. But darkness means nothing to a Venusian. You Earthmen play a strange game with cardboard rectangles. To use its language, Director Barrow, I have an ace in the hole."

Tar Norn sat down again and folded his six-fingered hands quite calmly. Light from the ceiling overhead seemed to cast a malignant glow on his dead-white scalp.

"Your daughter, Director," he continued. "If you wish to see her again, you will give me a ship, your *fastest* ship."

There was a moment of dead, utter silence. Then Director Barrow leaned over the desk and flicked the key of the communicator. "Control? Get my—get Leah Barrow at once. Ring her room. If no answer there, get my housekeeper. This is Director Barrow."

"Your fastest ship," repeated the Venusian. "Well stocked with supplies. Enough to take me to—to a place in the Asteroid belt. I shall be too late now to carry out my original plans on Ganymede."

The office door opened and Captain Wayne came in, followed by Roger Corey. Their eyes widened as they saw the Venusian. Wayne's hand darted toward his holster, then relaxed as he saw Mart's blaster trained on the pirate.

He faced Director Barrow and saluted.

"Captain," Barrow ordered, "you will form a search party at once—every available man and means. We must search all of Callisto within—" he made a rapid mental calculation "—about fifty miles. You will be searching for my daughter."

The captain stiffened. Before he could reply the carrier wave hummed and a feminine voice, that of an elderly woman, came over the communicator. "Director Barrow? Leah isn't here. I looked in her room and her bed is disarranged as though she left suddenly. She always makes it herself as soon as she gets up."

"Anything to point to when she left, Mrs. Andrews?"

"Not exactly, sir. The alarm was set for six and it was still buzzing. Her bed isn't very mussed; it looks like she got up again almost right after she retired. I don't understand."

Director Barrow's face was bleak. His voice sounded like the drip of water from melting ice. "Clothing?" he asked.

"Her lightweight spacesuit is gone. Apparently she put it on over her sleeping pajamas, for they aren't here. Is there anything I can do, sir? I'm worried; she hasn't ever—"

"That will be all, Mrs. Andrews," Barrow replied. "I'll let you know if there is anything."

He turned to Captain Wayne. "Use this set, Captain. Get Communications to send out a general alarm and assembly. You can make all necessary arrangements right here."

Wayne crossed to the communicator, and began to issue rapid instructions.

"Tell them to hurry," the Venusian cut in mockingly. "They have until nine-thirty o'clock."

Mart Wells glanced fearfully at the dial of the chronometer. It was eight-forty now. He turned and caught the Director's glance. "*The timer!*" he said grimly. "Captain Wayne said it was missing from the wrecked ship. He must have—"

The Venusian was grinning. "Exactly. The timer. And a pound of uranite. That gives you fifty minutes to search Callisto. It would be wiser to spend the time getting a ship ready for me instead."

The silence of the office was broken only by the low voice of Captain Wayne giving orders into the communicator. Abruptly he turned to his superior. His face was white.

"Search is on, sir. But if he isn't lying, there's a chance in a million. Less than an hour, and the area to be covered is—"

Barrow was looking straight ahead, and not a muscle of his face moved until he spoke. "I'm afraid he isn't bluffing. No reason why he should be. Leah is gone and the timer is gone. And a pirate ship would have uranite."

"The ship?" asked Tar Norn. "It will take some time to fuel it and—"

Director Barrow's voice was positive. "There will be no ship for you, Tar Norn."

Roger Corey's voice cut in, jerkily. "Let me work on him, sir. Me and Wayne. Maybe we can make him talk."

Barrow shook his head. "No use, Corey. Venusians don't mind pain as much as Earthmen. They almost like it. You could take him apart, and he wouldn't talk."

The pirate's smile faded. "It will take half an hour to prepare the ship, Director Barrow. Better not stall too long."

Mart said, his voice urgent. "But, sir, *Leah*! What's one pirate compared to—"

Barrow's face was granite-like. "He's killed hundreds of people. If we release him, he'll kill hundreds more. One life cannot weigh against that. Corey, take him away. Lock him up until the next ship leaves for Earth."

Mart's fists were clenched, his fingernails biting into the palms. But he knew Barrow was right; that he couldn't possibly take any other course and be worthy of his post. One life couldn't weigh against the many lives that meeting the pirate's terms would mean. That was where Tar Norn had miscalculated. A Venusian didn't understand responsibility to society, nor any higher ideal than self-interest.

Tar Norn tossed the wig and glasses to the floor as Corey took his arm. His pupil-less eyes seemed to glow with anger.

"You won't murder your own daughter, Director. This is a bluff. But mine isn't. She dies at nine-thirty unless you find her. I swear that by the *Eternal Varga*."

Mart cursed. Fists balled, he lunged toward the Venusian. Barrow put a hand on his arm. "Don't, Wells. That's up to the Interplanetary Council."

"But he's *not* bluffing," Mart raved. "Leah will surely die at nine-thirty. That damned oath. *Varga*. It's the only thing a Venusian is afraid of. He isn't—" His voice broke.

Corey started off with the Venusian.

Barrow said, "Yes, he's telling the truth. But we have some time yet. Maybe the search—"

Mart strode to the window and looked out so the others wouldn't see his face. Less than three-quarters of an hour to search all of Callisto within a radius of fifty miles!

Through the pane he saw figures in groups of three searching the streets and buildings of Comprotown. That part of the search wouldn't be difficult. But the hills and the caves, and with only two autogiros. If she was there, out of sight in one of the caves, where the cruising ships couldn't see her....

Her father was right, but—The picture of Leah Barrow, smiling as he had last seen her, seemed to blur out the view from the window. Her impertinent little tilted nose, the soft tempting contours of her lips, the deep blueness of her eyes.

He whirled from the window and began pacing the floor, trying to think of something they could do that wasn't being done. Again at the communicator, Captain Wayne was barking questions.

"All available men and women are combing the town, sir," he reported, "with orders to break down any doors that are locked, to stop at nothing."

"And outside, Captain?"

"The two giros are our only real hope. But the men from the smelting plant are working afoot out of town. By nine-thirty they'll have covered a radius of about five miles."

Corey returned, slamming the door viciously behind him. "Maybe we could trick him, sir," he suggested. "Pretend we'll give him a ship if he'll—"

"A Venusian wouldn't trust his own mother," Barrow snapped. "He'd insist on taking off first and then radioing back where she is. And don't think he wouldn't check the fuel tanks."

"I wish you'd let me and Wayne work on him, anyway."

Director Barrow didn't answer.

Mart growled, "If Leah dies, I'm going to take that filthy pirate and—"

Wayne's voice was bitter. "Venusians can't help what they are. Blame the Earth council that sold them those ships. If they had used more sense, there wouldn't be a Venusian off Venus."

Mart nodded. If the council hadn't pulled that boner twenty years before, there would be no trouble with the Venusians.

Venusians were, compared to Earth standards, a strange combination of genius and idiocy. Brilliant mathematicians, they had no mechanical ingenuity whatever. Linguists who could speak any language fluently after hearing it a few hours, not one of them could create a child's wind-up toy. Knowing the laws of leverage, they constructed their buildings by manual labor alone. Able to operate any machine as long as it was in good working order, they couldn't as much as figure out how to repair a clogged fuel-line.

Even the pirates based on some of the bigger Asteroids had to depend upon a few renegade Earthmen to keep their ships in running order. And if one went blah away from base, it was a gone ship as far as they were concerned. Probably the trouble that had forced Tar Norn down on Callisto had been a minor matter that any Earthman could have taken in his stride. But to Tar Norn it meant a new ship or nothing.

The thought of ships reminded him of the freighters. "Cap," he asked Wayne, "the freighters been searched thoroughly?"

Wayne nodded. "Rocket tubes and all. Even broke open the ore drums. I presume you'll want them to clear on schedule?"

Director Barrow nodded. "The crews?" he asked. "In the search or standing by?"

"Standing by for departure as usual, Director. A few men one way or the other—"

Barrow nodded, glancing at the chronometer. Mart knew what he was thinking. Less than half an hour now. And, unless the searchers by some miracle found Leah Barrow, it would all be over before the ten o'clock clearance of the first freighter. And the freighters hadn't missed a clearance in ten years.

The carrier wave hummed again. "Central Communications reporting. Most searchers in the town have reported in. No results. Those outside reaching points three miles out."

The communicator faded. Mart clenched his fists against the futility of that search. Three miles! The strong Venusian, in the light gravity of Callisto, probably had eight or ten hours of darkness to carry his burden. He could easily have covered twenty to forty miles, in any direction. Possibly even more. And the chance of an autogiro—

Obviously, Wayne had been thinking the same thing. "He timed his arrival," he said bitterly. "He gave us less than an hour. He'd certainly have put her outside walking range within that length of time. And with all the caves around, thousands of them, would he have put her where a giro could spot anything?"

Mart glanced at Barrow. The Director was sitting as immobile as a statue. His eyes were closed and every muscle of his thin face was tense. Probably he was trying not to look at the chronometer on the wall. It was nine-fifteen.

The office door opened and three uniformed mechanics from the field stood in the doorway. The foremost of them saluted. "This entire building has been searched twice except this office. I presume—"

Director Barrow opened his eyes and stood up. "Don't presume anything. Search here, too."

The men came in and began a detailed but fruitless search. Nobody spoke until they left.

The chronometer said twenty minutes after nine now. Ten minutes to go, if the timer had been accurately set. But could it have been set wrong? Venusians were lousy mechanics. Maybe—

Mart became aware that he was holding his breath for the sound of a distant explosion. Yes, from whatever point Tar Norn could have hidden his hostage, the sound of a pound of uranite exploding would carry back to Comprotown.

He sat down at his desk again. In front of him were the signed clearance papers for the freighters. In half an hour he'd take out the papers for the first freighter. But before that half hour was up—

He twisted a pencil between his fingers, held himself rigid to keep from turning and looking at the chronometer again. It hadn't been over a minute since he sat down—why torture himself by looking again? But each minute now seemed both a flash and an eternity.

He turned over the sheaf of papers and drew a little square on the blank reverse side of the bottom one. That was Comprotown. He made a dot an inch or two away. That was the point where Tar Norn's ship had wrecked itself in landing.

He drew a line from the point to the square. That was Tar Norn coming in to the town. That would have been about ten hours ago.

Then, from the information about Callisto and Comprotown that had been in the papers in Tar Norn's ship, the pirate had found the home of the director. He would have had no trouble finding Leah's room. Venusians could see in the dark and walk as silently as cats. He would undoubtedly have drugged Leah into unconsciousness, probably without awakening her, since there had been no sign of a struggle. He'd put her into the lightweight spacesuit.

Why? Undoubtedly it indicated that she would be outdoors. During the Callisto day, it would have been unnecessary. But an unconscious Earthwoman would freeze to death in the cold dark period of Callisto's eclipse behind Big Jupe.

What then? The Venusian left, carrying her—

The Venusian had carried the drugged girl into the night.

He threw down the pencil and began to pace the room again. His muscles were tense from listening. How many minutes? He didn't want to know; dared not look.

But Tar Norn must have planned it all before he left the wrecked ship. Otherwise he wouldn't have taken the timer and—

Would he have rigged the time-bomb first, or after he had kidnapped Leah? And how? The timer itself would not have provided the concussion to set off the uranite. He'd have needed a battery, a spark-coil, and—

But Venusians weren't mechanics.

They didn't understand machines, or electricity, or even simple clockworks, brilliant as their strange minds were in other ways.

Tar Norn could have set the timer all right. For that matter, he could calculate an orbit and make settings for space flight. But he couldn't have made a time-bomb, even with the timer. He couldn't have rigged a circuit that would set off a cap! And, Mart realized suddenly, the timer itself would be an electrical—not a clockwork—gadget. Once disconnected from the now broken dynamo of the ship, Tar Norn couldn't have made it run at all!

A momentary surge of elation swept Mart. Tar Norn must have been bluffing! Then he remembered: a Venusian might murder his own family, but he would never swear to an untruth by the Eternal Varga. That one superstition, or religion, as they looked upon it, was binding beyond all else. And Tar Norn had sworn by that oath that Leah Barrows would die at nine-thirty unless—

Mart looked at the chronometer. It was twenty-six minutes past nine. He caught a glimpse of Director Barrow's face. It looked like the face of a dead man. Barrow had obviously given up all hope and waited only for the four minutes to pass.

The carrier wave hummed. All of them started, but the voice from the communicator merely reported, "All Comprotown reports in. All negative. Giros report nothing. Foot parties five miles out. Reports negative."

Three minutes to go. Mart could see by the attitude of the others that they were bracing themselves for the sound of an explosion. All of them had liked, or loved, Leah Barrows. Mart had a momentary vision of her again, and remembered the electric thrill that had run through him when she had placed her hand on his arm, just a few days ago, and told him that she did care for him, well, a little anyway—

But, if Tar Norn couldn't have rigged a time-bomb, how could he have arranged for Leah to die at nine-thirty?

He saw again the corpse-like face of the Director. Yes, they had all been wrong in thinking that nothing mattered to Barrow more than the schedules—*Schedules!* There had been departure schedules among the papers in Tar Norn's ship. Could he have—

With a sudden intake of breath that was almost a gasp, Mart whirled and ran to the communicator. The others looked at him, startled. Mart was yelling at the mike even before he got near enough to it to talk in a normal voice. "Control! Emergency! Get *Jupe Freighter One*! *Tell him not to test his tubes.* Not to touch a lever!"

Then he was racing out of the door and across the field to where the big ugly freighter was up on the racks over the blasting pits. He wasn't counting on that message through the communicator.

Out of breath, he hammered on the steel door and yanked at the handle until the pilot opened it from within.

"Hold everything," Mart yelled at him. "Don't try the test blasts!"

Whether Mart was right or wrong, there needn't be any hurry now, but he was already lowering himself into the ash-filled blasting pit under the rocket tubes of the freighter. Carefully, he groped among the ashes from previous blast-offs, ignored the light soft ash that flew up into his face.

A hand touched heavy cloth, and the other found smooth transpariplast, the helmet of a spacesuit. Gently, he lifted the unconscious body of Leah Barrow and handed her up to the men looking down from the rim of the pit.

Ten minutes later, back in the office, Leah was reacting to the antidote Doc Rogers had just administered. A glance at her face had told the medico that the drug had been Venusian tragweed.

Mart was still answering questions. "... Sure, Tar Norn knew that. Every ship in the system makes its trial blasts just half an hour before take-off. It's a fixed convention. Rocket captains do everything according to a rigid schedule. And we were looking for a time-bomb so we'd never think of the blasting pits. But Tar Norn couldn't have rigged a time-bomb. We didn't think of that when we found the timer was gone. He'd just thrown it away—"

Someone was wringing his hand, and he saw it was Director Barrow. "Mart!" Barrow's voice wasn't cold and distant now; all the ice had melted. "I can't begin to tell you how much—If there is any reward I can possibly offer you—"

Mart Wells grinned. "—unto your daughter and half of your kingdom, as they used to say in stories? Well, sir, I don't know what I'd do with half of Callisto, but as for the other part of it—"

He turned back to the awakening girl. Director Barrow's answer was cinched, of course, but Leah—? Well, he'd have to ask her again.

But probably she wasn't up to that just yet, even though her eyes were open now and she was smiling at him. He'd have to give her time, of course, before he asked her. Lots of time. Say, five minutes, or maybe three.

Milton Keynes UK
Ingram Content Group UK Ltd.
UKHW031147311024
450535UK00004B/123